ABOVE LAS VEGAS
ITS CANYONS AND MOUNTAINS

BY ROBERT CAMERON

**A NEW COLLECTION OF HISTORICAL AND
ORIGINAL AERIAL PHOTOGRAPHS**

TEXT BY JACK SHEEHAN

CAMERON AND COMPANY, SAN FRANCISCO, CALIFORNIA

LAS VEGAS STRIP

text on page 160

(opposite) **MOUNT CHARLESTON**

GRAND CANYON

(opposite) **HOOVER DAM**

text on page 160

TABLE OF CONTENTS

Such a book as this does not reach publication without more than the usual cooperation from many people.
So, for their encouragement and expertise, I thank the following:

Hatsuro Aizawa, Christine Anderson-Holzman, Madeleine Cassidy, Robert Eckstrand, Rick Eisenreich, Art Gallenson, John Goy,
Linda Henry, Tina Hodge, Richard Manoogian, Peter Michel, Patricia O'Grady, Karen Perea, Phitty Phan,
Carol Sheehan, Norman Sheehan, Dani Williams, Stephen Wynn and Alex Yeminidjian.

Special mention goes to pilots:
Jim Granquist, John Sullivan, Michael Johns, Tom Schaus, Eric Rebstock and Earl Leseberg.

For assistance in researching the historical aerial photography, acknowledgement is made
to the University of Nevada at Las Vegas for pages 8, 10, 12, 14, 16.

The National Aeronautics and Space Administration, Ames Research Center, for pages 64, 92, 156.

CAMERON AND COMPANY

543 Howard Street   San Francisco, California 94105 USA   (415) 777-5582

Library of Congress Catalog Number:96-85987
ABOVE LAS VEGAS, ITS CANYONS AND MOUNTAINS ISBN: 0-918684-54-4
©1996 by Robert W. Cameron and Company, Inc. All rights reserved.

First printing, 1996

Book design by
JANE OLAUG KRISTIANSEN

Color Processing by the New Lab, San Francisco. Cameras by Pentax. Helicopters by Sundance, Las Vegas.
Typography by What a Beautiful Setting and Minnowillo, San Francisco.
Printed in Hong Kong.

Riding shotgun in a Bell Jet Ranger helicopter over the Las Vegas Strip, I turn back to observe a distinguished older gentleman in sportcoat and ascot, balancing a heavy camera on a gyro-stabilizer out the window. His nimble body is positioned much like any craftsman at his table, all limbs and senses involved in the task of completing his work. In this case, it is capturing the precise image on film that he's had in his mind's eye all along. The photographer will argue with me later that what he does with his camera from the sky is not art. I'll argue that it is.

As you graze through the following pages, decide for yourself whether Robert Cameron or I have the more convincing argument.

Collaborating on this book reinforced my love for Las Vegas, some 20 years after settling here, and left me more intrigued than ever with this percolating, dynamic, and endlessly original city.

Most people settle in Las Vegas for a good reason. Mine was that I had to get away — from a job and a girlfriend and a city that didn't seem to need me anymore. I was in my 20s then and I knew I wanted to be a writer, but it wasn't a literary siren that called me to the desert. Rather it was total diversion, 24 hours a day, with gambling and golf courses and girls to get my mind off matters, that lured me away from the Pacific Northwest, down 1100 miles of torn-up two-lane highway, to my eventual destiny.

The drive into this desert requires dodging jackrabbits and burros and cattle, who will stare you down as you approach at 75 miles per hour, as if to say, "Go ahead and run over me. I'll wreck your car out here on one of the loneliest roads in America and then see if you can get out alive!"

But arrive I did, on a balmy January day in 1976, and when I phoned my mother from an off-Strip fleabag and told her I thought I had found my new home — Las Vegas — she paused for a long moment, and said, "But what will I tell your father?"

I took the inevitable dealing job at a downtown hotel — the daunting 9 p.m. to 5 a.m. shift — as a way to make rent while magazine editors from coast to coast rejected my submissions. And I came to learn about Las Vegas from the inside out, from the belly of the beast, if you will.

That summer I'd sleep until about two-thirty in the afternoon, then awaken to temperatures between 105-115 degrees. Staggering out onto the balcony of my apartment, I'd stare at the swimming pool that was too hot to swim in, much less lie beside, then retire to the relative darkness of the living room, where I would read the morning paper, knowing that the news wasn't news anymore — it was already half a day outdated. I found it all rather disorienting.

Although I didn't relish that job, or that blur of time, I look back at it now with a surreal splendor, through an incandescent rear-view mirror that shows not the road I actually traveled, but a highway from another place, from another map, from another life. Francis Ford Coppola captured the setting perfectly in his film *One From the Heart*, when he showed a collection of misfits and Felliniesque characters dancing and reveling in the streets of the downtown Las Vegas intersection called Glitter Gulch.

On my 15-minute breaks from dealing, I'd lean against a trash basin outside the casino and watch the faces passing by. Each was so distinct, bathed as it was in the fluorescent light from the 45 miles of neon that wraps itself around the casino core. Those people had all come to this unlikely patch of earth for a good reason, just as I had. For a variety of other motives illustrated in this volume, they've never stopped coming.

In my case, Las Vegas was the perfect crash-pad for a writer, with its bold landscapes and its eclectic blend of schemers and dreamers whose stories are as vivid and bizarre as the backdrop. Moviemakers are magnetized by the city, and no fewer than a dozen first-rate feature films — from the *Godfather Part 2*, to *The Electric Horseman*, to *Bugsy*, to *Casino*, to *Melvin and Howard*, to *Leaving Las Vegas* (something I'll never permanently do) — have added dimension to the collective awareness of the town. Perhaps no city on earth brings a quicker smile of recognition to people on every continent than Las Vegas.

So it was high time that the foremost aerial photographer in the world, a man who has been celebrating landscapes and seascapes from the sky for 35 years by preserving incredible images shot out of the open door or windows of jazzy helicopters and fixed-wing aircraft, would aim his lens on Las Vegas and its spectacular surroundings. Robert Cameron, a spry 85-year-old, certainly took his time getting around to documenting this place, but his excuse was that he was busy capturing other great cities and geographic wonders. His bibliography of "*Above*" books include *Paris, New York, London, Washington (D.C.),* his hometown of *San Francisco* three times, *Yosemite, Carmel-Monterey-Big Sur, Tahoe-Reno, Seattle, Chicago, Mackinac, Los Angeles, San Diego* and *Hawaii*. Las Vegas is honored to be joining their company. And so am I.

How did Cameron pick 1996 as the year to document Las Vegas? "It just seemed like the right time," he says. "But I must say after seeing all the spectacular sights, I perhaps should have come earlier. The variety is just astounding."

Cameron allowed me to take two excursions with him — sun up and sun down — to see firsthand many of the images set forth on these pages, and to get a peek at his method. My first flight, a chopper hop down the Las Vegas Strip at night, drew a big laugh from Cameron. "What a baptism!" he chuckled. "You're spoiled forever."

Through our headphones, we chatted about the relevance to our project of certain structures along the Strip, but Cameron had done his homework. Although he knew in general what he wanted, he was always hopeful of being surprised by some fabulous unexpected landscape or geological formation. Unlike the modern-day photographer, with his propensity to shoot five rolls of film to capture that one precious shot, Bob would often take just one photograph of a site we knew would be included. When I inquired about that, he borrowed a line from his late friend Ansel Adams. "Photographically I am a fly fisherman," he said. "I do not need to dynamite the stream."

To some, it may seem that hanging out of helicopters is a risky way for an octogenarian to make a living. A few years ago, Cameron was shooting *Above Yosemite*, and he had captured an image of climbers pasted like flies halfway up a 3,300-foot sheer rock wall. Later, down on the valley floor, one of the climbers said: "So you were the guy photographing us from a chopper; man, I wouldn't do that for all the tea in China."

Cameron replied that he wouldn't be scaling El Capitan anytime soon, either.

Danger, to an aficionado, is a relative term.

What strikes one in observing Bob Cameron's photos of the southern Nevada area and its surrounding canyons and mountains, is the cohesive blending of man and nature, and how even when man's presence was most intrusive, it doesn't offend when viewed from above. Take Hoover Dam, for instance. From the sky, this white wedge interrupting the even blue flow of the Colorado River appears as natural and wonderful as the water that provides hydroelectric power and nourishment to the valley below.

And the Luxor pyramid, located right next to the Excalibur kingdom, across the street from the New York-New York megalopolis and the MGM Grand theme park. There's no logic to how this hyperbolic architecture raised to the umpteenth power all works together, but somehow it does. Then get out of town, and revel in the rose and crimson of Red Rock Canyon, or explore the white peaks of Mount Charleston, or go east to the cathedral spires of Bryce Canyon and Zion, and you'll grasp the vastness and antiquity of the region. These wonders were formed over millions of years, and yet the Strip is just 50 years old. Geologists fear not; mankind has barely made a dent in any of it.

The Las Vegas area, both geographically and economically, is one of extremes, to be sure. Las Vegas has been the fastest growing city in the country for two decades. The county population surpassed 1 million residents in 1995, having jumped from well under 500,000 just 20 years ago. The school district is also setting growth records, nearly doubling in size in the last 10 years. And the oldster population boom is keeping pace with the youngsters, as over half of the 150,000 retirees have lived in Las Vegas less than 10 years. They were lured here by lush retirement communities and the attractive Nevada tax climate. The convention industry also continues its steady surge with record numbers of conventions and attendees, two of which brought over 130,000 delegates to town in 1996.

Indeed the city has almost become respectable — we shudder at the thought — so much so that *Time* magazine not long ago did a cover story calling Las Vegas the All-American City. Mobster and showgirl movies, once the staple of Las Vegas, are even making room for titles like *Honey, I Blew Up the Baby*, and *Vegas Vacation*, in which Chevy Chase and his film family of dweebs come to town for some wholesome fun.

Bugsy's bullet-riddled body is rolling over in its grave.

Although the city's image may be undergoing a massage, the undeniable fact is that Las Vegas gets more intriguing, and certainly more picturesque, as we march toward the millennium.

And for that reason, Bob Cameron has every intention of returning in a few years to chronicle all the changes from above. I hope he asks me along again.

— Jack Sheehan

THEN AND NOW

(*above*) **DOWNTOWN LAS VEGAS** in the late 1920s, prior to establishing its niche as an international entertainment and gambling mecca. The Union Pacific Railroad yard (foreground) recalls the city's origins as a whistlestop at the turn of the century. (*opposite*) Downtown today, some 70 years later, has evolved into a bustling area of gaming commerce and local politics. The passing trains hearken to an earlier day, when the rail line was the lifeblood of the community.

(*above*) **NEVADA SOUTHERN UNIVERSITY**, 1965. This tiny school, shortly to become the University of Nevada Las Vegas, benefited from the foresight of civic leaders, who parcelled 335 acres to accommodate future growth. (*opposite*) **UNLV** today, a school which has gained prominence from its national championship basketball team (1990) and its appraisal by *U.S. News and World Report* as " a rising star in higher education." In 1996, the university has 58 academic buildings, 19,500 students, and more than 600 faculty members.

(*above*) **JOE W. BROWN RACETRACK** (1964). This horseracing attraction would later receive national attention when it was developed into Las Vegas Country Club, the original host course for the PGA Tour. The Las Vegas Pro Celebrity Classic had a record million-dollar purse when it came to town in 1983. (*opposite*) **LAS VEGAS COUNTRY CLUB** was the first true country club in the city. Located in the heart of town, for years it defined country club living and social panache in a city desperately seeking an identity off the Strip.

(*above*) **McCARRAN FIELD AIRPORT** (1962). In that year, it handled 1.28 million passengers, just 4 percent of the current total. The tiny aircraft dotting the field speak as much about advances in aviation as they do the growth of Las Vegas as an international tourist destination. (*opposite*) Currently the 10th busiest airport in the United States, **McCARRAN INTERNATIONAL AIRPORT** ranks as the 16th busiest in the world. Since 1982, McCarran has doubled in average daily scheduled flights and tripled in passenger volume, handling 30 million travelers in 1995. The airport is currently completing a $100-million expansion and improvement.

(*above*) The south end of the **LAS VEGAS STRIP** in the early 1970s. The famous Stardust sign (center, left) and the Circus Circus tent were early signatures. (*opposite*) Nowadays, the ever-expanding and upgrading Strip has eye-catchers like Grand Slam Canyon (rounded purple building, far left) and the Stratosphere Tower standing tall and proud like an exclamation point at the end of the Strip.

CASINOS

(*left*) The billion-dollar **MGM GRAND**, with 5005 rooms and covering 112 acres, has dazzled the tourist market since its 1993 opening. It's the third time that owner Kirk Kerkorian has built the largest hotel in the world in Las Vegas. The Grand's first headliner was Barbra Streisand. (*right*) The **MGM GRAND ADVENTURES** was built on the site of the Tropicana Golf Course, and is a 33-acre theme park featuring rides, shows, themed streets, entertainment, restaurants, retail shops, and two wedding chapels. (*opposite*) **LUXOR**, owned and operated by Circus Circus Inc., brings ancient Egypt to the new Las Vegas. Shining from the apex of the pyramid is a 40-billion candlepower laser that beams 10 miles into space and is visible at cruising altitude from Los Angeles, about 275 miles away.

(*above*) **EXCALIBUR**, second only to its neighbor MGM Grand as the largest hotel in the world, is located just north of the Luxor and belongs to the same parent company, Circus Circus Inc. A medieval theme is carried throughout the property, which prides itself on affordability and its appeal to all ages. (*below*) Excalibur was repainted in richer tones a couple years after its 1990 opening, greatly enhancing its nocturnal luminescence.

The **TROPICANA** was labeled the "Tiffany of the Strip" upon its opening in 1957. Two years later, the hotel welcomed the famed *Folies Bergere*, which still packs the showroom four decades later. Nowadays, the Tropicana bills itself as "the Island of Las Vegas," and features a five-acre water theme park as its central attraction.

(*opposite*) Since the late 1980s, Strip construction has been frenetic. The latest editions under construction in early 1996 represented a new trend of large corporations linking arms on specific properties. **NEW YORK-NEW YORK**, a partnership between Primadonna and MGM Grand *(left)*; and **MONTE CARLO**, a collaboration with Circus Circus Inc. and Mirage Resorts Inc., bring two more glamorous international themes to the Strip. (*above and below*) The **ALADDIN** has a long and storied history on the south end of the Strip, with owners as varied as entertainer Wayne Newton and controversial billionaire Ginji Yasuda. The domed 7,000-seat Theater for Performing Arts opened with Neil Diamond in 1976.

(*left*) Site of the original MGM Grand, **BALLY'S LAS VEGAS** purchased the property in 1986 and now occupies the southeast corner of what was once billed "the busiest intersection in the country." Traffic-conscious Bally's has participated with the new MGM Grand in a monorail system and ushers guests into (and out of) the casino with a series of moving walkways. (*right*) Bally's bold color scheme is apropos for the heart of the Strip.

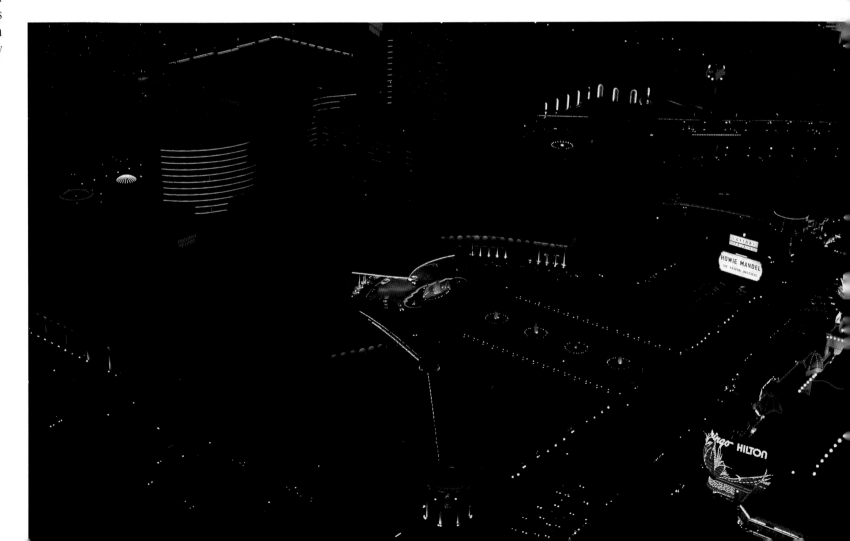

(*above and below*) **CAESARS PALACE** has been home to more international spectacles than any Strip hotel – from Muhammad Ali's last fight, to Evel Knievel's failed fountain jump, to world-class tennis and gymnastics. Its Forum Shops, north of the main entrance, provide the most exclusive and visually enhancing shopping experience on the Strip.

(*above*) Not quite "the place that Bugsy built" any-more, the **FLAMINGO HILTON** nevertheless carries on the name, the location, and the mystique associated with the notorious Benjamin Siegel. The first super resort on the Strip was acquired by the Hilton Hotels Corporation in 1970. (*below*) This view of Bally's, the Flamingo Hilton, Imperial Palace and Harrah's reflects Las Vegas nightlife at its most eclec-tic and vibrant. If you're looking for understatement, look elsewhere.

(*above*) Distinctive by its riverboat in the "front yard," **HARRAH'S** is independent from its chain, but carries on a successful gaming tradition started by the legendary Bill Harrah in Reno and Lake Tahoe. Harrah's was formerly the largest Holiday Inn in the country. **IMPERIAL PALACE** (right) has also succeeded by its great Strip location (across from Caesars) and strong private ownership. (*below*) Shortly after this photo was taken, it was announced that the **SANDS** tower would be imploded to make way for a billion dollar mega-hotel/convention complex. In its heyday, the Sands was party headquarters for Frank, Dean, Sammy, Joey, and Peter . . . aka The Rat Pack. Presidents Kennedy and Reagan also stayed there while in office.

(*above*) **RIO**, an off-Strip hotel-casino, has been a success story of the 90s. With savvy marketing, a strong Latin American carnival theme, and attractive all-suite accommodations, the Rio has been under nearly constant expansion since it opened. (*below*) Rio and the **GOLD COAST** (white building behind Rio), owned and operated by Barbary Coast's Michael Gaughan, have successfully integrated the local market with tourists seeking a diversion from the Strip. (*opposite*) The **SHERATON DESERT INN** is a complete resort hotel, with a wonderful spa, five tennis courts, and the best on-property golf course in the city. In recent years, the showroom has booked many classic headliners from years past to appeal to a mature clientele and high-rollers.

(*right*) **THE MIRAGE** opened in 1989 and immediately raised the stakes for operators up and down the Strip. With its rich marble interiors and lush tropical atmosphere, plus a $40-million volcano which erupts at regular intervals, the resort announced to the world that Las Vegas was a big-time, first-class destination city. (*below left*) The Mirage's **DOLPHIN POND** represented a political victory for owner Steve Wynn and an educational victory for Clark County schoolchildren and visitors who wish to learn more about our slippery brothers from the sea. (*below right*) The Mirage at night shimmers like a gold jewel, with its lustrous reflective exterior.

Next door to The Mirage, **TREASURE ISLAND** opened in 1993 and targeted a younger, more middle-class clientele than its big sister. Featuring a commercial and residential area called Buccaneer Bay Village, and a nightly harbor battle between a British man-o-war and the pirate ship *Hispanola*, Treasure Island's sea spectacle draws thousands of observers every night.

The **LAS VEGAS HILTON**, located next door to the Las Vegas Convention Center, has become a magnet for meetings, trade shows, and convention business. But it also has a rich past in the entertainment field, with headliners like Barbra Streisand, Liberace and, of course, Elvis, who for years drew fans to the Hilton from all over the world. A monument to The King still stands outside the showroom.

The **SAHARA HOTEL** (with Wet 'n Wild water park to the south) opened in 1952 and is noted for the many great entertainers who made their Las Vegas debut there: Mae West, Ann-Margret, Judy Garland, Liza Minelli, Paul Anka, Marlene Dietrich, and Johnny Carson. The Sahara sign is the world's tallest free-standing sign at 222 feet. The hotel was purchased in 1995 by William Bennett, the man given credit for the great success of Circus Circus.

(*above*) With more showrooms than any hotel in town, and the most varied entertainment mix (five distinctly different shows and 69 performances weekly), the **RIVIERA** draws a populous and diverse clientele. A former owner was tycoon Meshulem Riklis, who frequently booked his wife Pia Zadora into the showroom. (*below*) The **FRONTIER** sits on the site of the original Last Frontier, the first major hotel on the Las Vegas Strip. An ongoing labor strike has not sullied the patronage of Frontier guests, who enjoy the recent addition of mini-suites and a spruced-up casino.

(*above*) When **WET 'N WILD** water park opened next to the Sahara Hotel on the Strip in 1984, it sent a clear message to the world that children were welcome in a town often called the "adult Disneyland." With thrill rides and slides like Banzai Boggan and *Der Stuka* – the fastest and highest water chute in the world – the park has been packed since opening day. (*below*) On those blistering summer nights when the mercury lingers above 100 degrees until well after dark, Wet 'n Wild stays open until 11 p.m.

(*above*) **CIRCUS CIRCUS** opened in 1968, the fulfillment of an entrepreneurial dreamer named Jay Sarno. Featuring the world's finest acrobats, tightrope walkers, and flying trapeze artists, the hotel has been an amazing success story, and during the 1980s was the darling of Wall Street investors. **GRAND SLAM CANYON** (foreground), which opened in 1993, was Las Vegas' first amusement park. (*below*) Circus Circus at night has an almost extraterrestrial glow to it.

(*above and below*) Well situated on Convention Center Drive, the sprawling **STARDUST** has been a popular mainstay of the Strip for decades. Now capably managed by Boyd Gaming Corporation, its *Enter the Night* production show is one of the city's most popular. The Stardust also does a brisk convention business and has one of the world's largest and most respected sports books.

(*opposite*) The spectacular $550-million **STRATO-SPHERE TOWER** opened in April, 1996, and instantly became the talk of the town. Soaring to 1,149 feet, it is America's tallest free-standing observation tower and the tallest building west of the Mississippi. Helicopter skids frame the bottom of this fisheye-lens photo. (*right*) The Stratosphere looms over the valley in much the same manner that the Space Needle dominates Seattle. (*below right*) Thrill-seekers can joy ride more than 100 stories above the ground on two of the world's highest rides: the Let It Ride roller coaster; and Big Shot, which shoots riders 160 feet into the air and allows them to experience G forces of up to four and less than zero. (*below*) The Las Vegas night sky will never be the same with the Stratosphere in place.

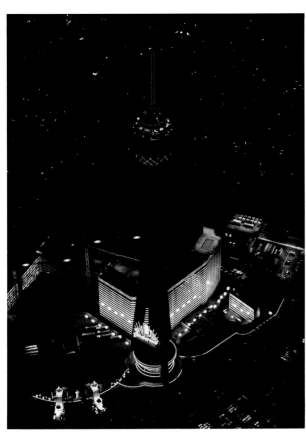

DOWNTOWN

(*above*) This section of **DOWNTOWN** Las Vegas is the seed from which the city grew. A land auction was held on May 15, 1905, and bidders were enticed from Salt Lake City and Los Angeles by the offer of a rebate on their rail ticket if they purchased a lot. A choice corner of downtown could be purchased for $600. What do you suppose it's worth today? (*opposite*) The **CALIFORNIA HOTEL** (foreground) and its neighbors all benefit from the $70-million **FREMONT STREET EXPERIENCE**. The elaborate space frame (center) running down Fremont Street is home to a computerized laser show which has 2.1 million lights, a 540,000-watt sound system, and is capable of producing over 65,000 color combinations. Most signficantly, the Experience has cleaned up and unified downtown Las Vegas and dramatically increased tourist activity.

(*opposite*) **DOWNTOWN** Las Vegas at night, often referred to as Glitter Gulch, is perhaps the most intensely lit patch of real estate on earth. The sprawling lights of the city beyond were all sparked by the legalized gambling that took place in these casinos. (*above*) **LADY LUCK, HORSESHOE, FREMONT,** and **FREMONT STREET EXPERIENCE** are visible in the foreground, blending smoothly with the bank buildings and private offices that comprise a bustling downtown. (*below*) Yet another view of majestic dowtown Las Vegas.

(*above*) **FIESTA** Casino Hotel (foreground) opened in 1994 on North Rancho Drive and further proved that Las Vegas could embrace neighborhood casinos. Featuring an Old Mexico theme, its restaurants specialize in Mexican and Southwestern food. (background) **TEXAS STATION** is the third leg of the Station Properties which include Palace Station, Boulder Station, and Sunset Station. Like its neighbor, Texas Station has a strong local patronage, and draws its share of curious visitors from the Lone Star state. (*below*) **SANTA FE** broke new ground for neighborhood casinos in 1991 when it was built on North Rancho, not far from the base of Mount Charleston. A terrific ice-skating arena on the property has been training ground for the likes of Olympic gold medalists Oksana Baiul and Viktor Petrenko.

(*above*) **BOOMTOWN**, southwest of Las Vegas at the Blue Diamond Road exit off I-15, opened in 1994 with an Old West mining-town theme. As happens with many new casinos in a bullish economy, its 300 rooms are expanding to over 1000. (*below*) Hot Las Vegas got a whole lot cooler with the opening of the **HARD ROCK HOTEL AND CASINO** in March, 1995. The $100-million property welcomes visitors to pass under a 90-foot-tall Fender Stratocaster guitar, and a 1400-seat live concert venue hosts music stars like Melissa Etheridge and Hootie and the Blowfish.

(*left*) The **SHOWBOAT** opened on Boulder Highway in 1954 and has found its niche by offering great buffets, an elaborate bingo parlor, and the world's largest bowling center with 106 lanes. Each year it hosts the nationally televised Showboat Invitational for the Professional Bowlers Association. (*right*) Las Vegas' most popular off-Strip casino is **SAM'S TOWN**, also on Boulder Highway. The main attraction is Mystic Falls Park, a 25,000-square-foot park under an atrium ceiling. It features a laser-light and water show, plus waterfalls, brooks, cobblestone footpaths, and lifelike birds and animals. (*opposite*) **GOLD STRIKE INN & CASINO** is just three miles from Lake Mead and an easy stop for Hoover Dam visitors. The property opened in 1957 and has expanded four times through the years.

A COMMUNITY MATURES

The **LAS VEGAS CONVENTION CENTER** is the second largest convention and trade show facility in the United States. The building contains 1.3 million square feet of exhibit and meeting space, a kitchen that can cater a banquet for 12,000, and nearly 100 meeting rooms. In 1995, there were 2,826 conventions in Clark County which were attended by more than 2.9 million delegates. For several years, Las Vegas has been considered one of the three most attractive convention cities in the country.

(*left*) **LIED DISCOVERY CHILDREN'S MU-SEUM** is an award-winning architectural design by Antoine Predock, and a tribute and cultural offering to the children of Las Vegas. A totally hands-on museum, all exhibits are also interactive, encouraging children to handle, climb over, walk through, and question thoroughly their function and purpose. (*below left*) The colorful **COMMUNITY COLLEGE** of **SOUTHERN NEVADA WEST CHARLESTON** campus. (*below right*) CCSN's **CHEYENNE** campus. The white building is the **WEST CHARLESTON LIBRARY.**

(*above*) **CIMARRON MEMORIAL HIGH SCHOOL**, at Smoke Ranch Road and Tenaya, is a relatively new addition to the fastest growing school district in the United States. (*below*) The **LAS VEGAS ACADEMY OF INTERNATIONAL STUDIES AND PERFORMING ARTS** trains students in music and the fine arts and has developed an outstanding reputation in the community. (*opposite*) The **CLARK COUNTY GOVERNMENT CENTER** centralizes agencies previously situated in 12 different locations into a single government services agency, and perhaps just as importantly demonstrates how far local architecture has advanced since national art critics used to mercilessly lambaste the neon gaudiness of Las Vegas.

(*above*) The **GRANT SAWYER BUILDING**, named for a popular former Nevada governor and Democratic Party political leader, houses several state government offices, including that of current Gov. Robert Miller when he is in Las Vegas. (*opposite*) **LAS VEGAS CITY HALL** is home to the Metropolitan Police Department and held an international competition for artists who competed to display their work on the outer face of the building.

(*above*) The new **GALLERIA MALL**, on Sunset Road off I-95, demonstrates the arching growth of Las Vegas into all corners of the valley. The mall has 110 specialty stores and four anchors, Robinsons-May, J.C. Penney, Mervyn's, and Dillard's. (*below*) The **MEADOWS MALL**, opened in 1978 off West Charleston and the Las Vegas Expressway, has 73 stores spread over two levels and is traditionally the city's busiest mall.

(*above*) Yes, Las Vegas requires medical care just like the rest of the world. **SIERRA HEALTH SERVICES**, an HMO, (white building, front) is just down the street from **SUNRISE MOUNTAIN VIEW HOSPITAL** (*center left*) an 80-bed facility specializing in acute care, which opened in January, 1996. (*below*) The **NORTH LAS VEGAS AIRPORT** was opened on December 7, 1941, the day the Japanese bombed Pearl Harbor. It is used primarily for private aircraft and flight instruction, and has 160 enclosed hangars and 201 shade hangars.

(*opposite*) **CASHMAN FIELD CENTER**, which houses trade shows and a variety of civic gatherings, is also home to the Las Vegas Stars, the AAA affiliate of the San Diego Padres. In a city notorious for being lukewarm to professional sports teams, the Stars have drawn excellent crowds since 1983. (*above*) **SAM BOYD STADIUM**, named for a late Las Vegas gaming legend and avid UNLV supporter, holds 31,318 and is home to the university's football team. The stadium saw its biggest crowd in recent years, 41,500, not at a ball game, but at a recent Grateful Dead concert.

(*above*) **SUNRISE COUNTRY CLUB** is a 54-hole affordable private course developed by Senior PGA Tour star Jim Colbert. It is probably best known for having given up one of only two sub-60 rounds in PGA Tour history, when Chip Beck recorded a 59 during the 1991 Las Vegas Invitational. For the feat, Beck was awarded $500,000 by the Hilton Hotels Corporation, with another half million designated for his favorite charity. (*opposite*) **SHERATON DESERT INN**

COUNTRY CLUB has the most history of any course in Las Vegas, having been home to the Tournament of Champions from the early 1950s to the late 1960s. Palmer, Nicklaus, Snead, and company all won titles at the D.I. and were dramatically paid their winnings in wheelbarrows heaping with silver dollars. The celebrity pro-am drew the likes of Hope, Crosby, and Sinatra. A recent $8 million renovation has the course looking better, and playing tougher, than ever before.

(*opposite*) The starkness of a golf course blooming out of the desert is no more apparent than at **CRAIG RANCH** in North Las Vegas. An active municipal course which favors beginners and intermediate players, it has 11,000 trees and perhaps the smallest greens in the state. (*above*) **SPANISH TRAIL COUNTRY CLUB**, became just the second exclusive country club in Las Vegas, and the first on the west side of town. It is as notable for the exquisite homes which border the fairways as for the golf. Unlike most desert courses, it has undulating fairways, a number of attractive and intimidating water features, and fast, bent-grass greens.

(*above*) **FLOYD LAMB STATE PARK**, northwest of Las Vegas, is one of nature's ways of saying that humans are welcome in this somewhat barren region. Formerly called Tule Springs, this 2040-acre park offers fishing and hosts family picnics, and has long been a placid oasis amidst stark surroundings. In contrast to these peaceful environs is the **LAS VEGAS GUN CLUB** (lower right), just across the street. (*opposite*) **LAS VEGAS PAIUTE RESORT** offers 36 holes just 20 minutes north of the Strip. **NU-WAV-KAIV** (Snow Mountain) and **TAV-AI-KAIV** (Sun Mountain) are challenging Pete Dye designs that received national acclaim from the top golf magazines. Notice the Indian designs in the foreground.

A NASA photograph, taken from the earth's atmosphere, of North Las Vegas and Nellis Air Force Base on June 3, 1992. Shadow Creek Country Club (the square at left) and the Nellis Air Force Base Golf Course (slightly right and below) photograph red in infrared photography.

NELLIS AIR FORCE BASE is a proud and welcome participant in the Las Vegas community. The base took its name in 1950 from William H. Nellis, an area resident who had died in World War II. Today it is the home to the 57th Wing of the United States Air Force. Among the squadrons reporting to the 57th Operations Group is the 414th Combat Training Squadron, called Red Flag, which was immortalized in the movie *Top Gun*. The U.S. Air Force Demonstration Squadron, better known as the Thunderbirds, plans and presents precision aerial maneuvers to exhibit the capabilities of modern high-performance aircraft and the high degree of professional skill required to operate and maintain these aircraft. Many area residents feel the Thunderbirds put on the best show in Las Vegas.

The **MORMON TEMPLE** of the Church of Jesus Christ of Latter Day Saints was dedicated in December, 1989, at the base of Sunrise Mountain and is a source of great pride and worship for the extensive Mormon population in the valley.

The highly developed East Charleston/Lamb Boulevard sector of Las Vegas, spreading out to the mantel of Sunrise Mountain in the background.

(*above*) The upscale and affluent west side of Las Vegas, which was virtually undeveloped 25 years ago, is exemplified by the lush **CANYON GATE COUNTRY CLUB** community (center) and, to its left, **THE LAKES** residential development. (*below*) Further westside growth is seen in the **PECCOLE RANCH** community (upper right). The Sahara West branch of the Las Vegas-Clark County Library district is the white building to its left.

(*above*) The three golf courses that are part of **SUN CITY SUMMERLIN** (Palm Valley, Highland Falls, and Eagle Crest) form interesting geometric patterns from the sky. Two-time U.S. Open champion Billy Casper was involved in the design of the courses, which are suited to the games of active seniors. (*below*) The **TOURNAMENT PLAYERS CLUB** at **SUMMERLIN** complex revolves around Center Circle. This burgeoning and affluent community has become one of the most desirable in southern Nevada. A library and performing arts center are in the middle of the circle. To the far right, center, is the clubhouse and driving range of TPC Summerlin, rated the second best course in Nevada behind Shadow Creek. Each year since 1992 the course plays host to the Las Vegas Invitational, one of the richest events on the PGA Tour. TPC members include four-time Cy Young winner Greg Maddux, PGA star Robert Gamez, and Senior PGA leading money winner Jim Colbert.

(*above*) **TPC SUMMERLIN**, during winter when the Bermuda grass is dormant. The golf course lots are under rapid development, and keeping up with the Joneses is not easy. The white house (lower center) is 17,000 square feet. The three lakes (upper center) mark the demanding final three holes of the course, where the Las Vegas Invitational is decided each year. A few holes of Angel Park Golf Course can be seen just right of Rampart Boulevard. (*below*) Another view of the **SUN CITY SUMMERLIN** golf courses, with Lone Mountain in the background. Earnest A. Becker Middle School is on the left and William R. Lummis Elementary School is on the right, foreground.

(*above*) **SPANISH TRAIL COUNTRY CLUB** (background) has 27 holes and when it was developed in 1984 quickly became the place to live in Las Vegas. For several years it was played by the PGA Tour. Foreground center is the sprawling complex belonging to homegrown tennis star Andre Agassi, winner of Wimbledon and the U.S. and Australian Open tennis championships. Agassi and his mate Brooke Shields are not shy about being seen around town, patronizing their favorite dining establishments. (*below*) The booming northwest corridor was nearly vacant back when ace helicopter pilot Tom Schaus, who was at the controls for many of these pictures, built his large house (center front). Now sizable homes are everywhere the eye can see.

(*above*) Pretty houses all in a row describes this section of **GREEN VALLEY**, a planned community in neighboring Henderson. (*below*) **CANYON GATE COUNTRY CLUB**, an affluent golf course community in northwest Las Vegas, has played host to the LPGA Tour and the annual Robert Gamez Charity Classic, which brings PGA Tour stars and celebrities to town.

(*above*) **DESERT SHORES**, an upscale development in northwest Las Vegas, came to fruition in the early 1980s, when southern Nevada's residential growth rate reached national highs. (*below*) Another view of **SUN CITY SUMMERLIN**, which was successfully patterned after the Del Webb community in Arizona.

(*above*) **HENDERSON** looking north reveals **BLACK MOUNTAIN GOLF AND COUNTRY CLUB** in the center and the **BASIC MAGNESIUM PLANT**, which was instrumental in aiding America's war effort in 1941 and fueled the early growth of Henderson. (*below*) **GREEN VALLEY** looking to the northeast, with Wigwam Avenue bisecting. Two golf courses available for public play, Legacy Golf Club (center) and Wildhorse (far left) can be seen.

(*above*) Yes, there is plenty of water in this desert. **THE LAKES** residential community offers a variety of luxurious homes (note the number of private swimming pools) and is headquarters to Citibank's credit-card processing plant. (*below*) A more expansive view of The Lakes (background).

HELICOPTER TOUR

(*above*) Emerging as an industrial site at the beginning of World War II, **HENDERSON** has grown into one of Nevada's largest cities. The community emphasizes family activities and recreation (note the baseball diamonds throughout) and is quickly tiring of its tag as Las Vegas' little sister. The **HENDERSON CONVENTION CENTER** and civic complex can be seen in center photo. (*opposite*) Another view of Henderson and Legacy Golf Club.

(*opposite*) **RAINBOW GARDENS GEOLOGICAL PRESERVE**, just north of Lake Las Vegas. How could man ever approach the artistry that it took nature a half million years to compose? (*above*) These reservoirs near the industrial area south of town resemble an artist's palette, awaiting a paintbrush to sprinkle a variety of hues over the stark, gun-metal landscape.

(*above*) A riddle page. Find the desert wildlife roaming near the banks of Lake Mead. Give up? All right, that's a desert bighorn sheep (left), posing for the camera; and a wandering burro (right) wondering why everyone would crowd into Las Vegas when there's so much open space where he resides. (*opposite*) It's not easy to get **BOULDER CITY, LAKE MEAD,** and **HOOVER DAM** (far right) all in the same picture. You just have to fly high enough.

(*above*) An abandoned **GOLD MINE** (center, left) on the outskirts of the Grand Canyon still has gold in it, but is now owned by the government. (*opposite*) Entering the **GRAND CANYON.** When Francisco de Coronado, the first white man to discover the canyon, saw it in 1540 he thought he had discovered the Seven Cities of Gold.

(*above*) The **GRAND CANYON** is 277 miles long, averages 10 miles in width at the heart of the canyon, and is a mile deep. Explorer John Wesley Powell described the free-standing temples and buttes as "the leaves of a great stony book." (*opposite*) According to the time of day, colors and shapes change dramatically in the canyon.

(*opposite*) The upper two-thirds of the canyon walls are comprised of alternating layers of shale, sandstone, and lime deposited between 600 million and 250 million years ago. (*above*) Erosion creates masterpieces everywhere you look in the **GRAND CANYON**. A formation's relative position from bottom to top assists geologists in determining its age.

(*above*) A Sundance Helicopter takes a rest from its chores, as do picnickers enjoying a lunch and a spectacular vista. (note: This is the only non-aerial photograph in the book.) (*opposite*) A rare instance of shooting upwards in the **GRAND CANYON**.

(*opposite*) The insignificance of man against the vastness of nature is represented by this speck-like speedboat racing down the Colorado River near the Grand Canyon. (*above*) The hearty Colorado snakes its way through the mile-deep canyon.

A NASA photo of the **GRAND CANYON** and **LAKE MEAD**, taken with a hand-held camera on April 14, 1993, during Shuttle Mission 56. The Canyon is at lower left in photo and the lake is in the lower left corner.

(*above*) The shoreline of **LAKE MEAD** provides some intriguing shapes from the air, such as the monster's head shown here (clue: start with the gaping mouth and you'll see it.) (*below*) "The camera sometimes sees more than I do," says Bob Cameron. This photo was taken at one of those times.

LAKE MEAD

OVERTON, Nevada, a Mormon community established in the 1880s, is situated on the northern edge of Lake Mead. (*opposite*) Just west of Overton is **VALLEY OF FIRE STATE PARK**, a geological wonder with rock formations over a billion years old. Over tens of millions of years, lofty sand dunes were carved by wind into fantastic formations called fossil dunes.

(*opposite*) Roads weave through **VALLEY OF FIRE STATE PARK**, a popular tourist attraction for those drawn to the brilliant colors and rock formations, and the well-preserved Indian petroglyphs (rock carvings) drawn centuries ago by Native Americans. (*above*) Exposure of sediments to air over the centuries caused many of the iron compounds in the sand to rust, creating a mosaic of reds, purples, pinks, and lavenders throughout the park.

97

(*above*) A portion of **LAKE MEAD** resembles a narrow version of a map of the United States. The country's largest man-made lake is distinctive by its many fingers, nooks, inlets, and coves. Lake Mead is part of America's National Park System, and with 1.3 million acres of land and another 200,000 acres of water within its boundaries, it is the third largest park in the contiguous states. (*opposite*) **CALLVILLE BAY RESORT** on Lake Mead has 607 boat slips and a trailer village with 97 sites.

ECHO BAY RESORT (center), with Overton and Valley of Fire State Park in the background, offers a 339-slip marina, with a restaurant, motel, and sizable trailer village. Sport fishermen are drawn from throughout the world to challenge the bass, striped bass, rainbow trout, channel catfish, and bluegill found in the lake.

(*above*) **TEMPLE BAR RESORT**, on the eastern side of Lake Mead, is another full-service marina.
(*opposite*) **LAKE MEAD RESORT** is the entry point to the lake for most Las Vegas residents and visitors
driving from the heart of town. It has a store, restaurant, motel, and 728-slip marina.

(*opposite*) A western section of **LAKE MEAD**. Saddle Island is in the center and **LAS VEGAS BAY MARINA**, with 745 slips, is at far right. (*above*) Boats cruise to the brim of **HOOVER DAM**. A machine-gun nest was located in the hillside (left) to protect the Dam from saboteurs during World War II.

(*above*) **BOULDER CANYON**, the narrow passageway (upper center), was the first choice for the dam site, but was nixed by geologists because Black Canyon, the eventual site, had better rock formations and required a shorter special rail line. (*opposite*) The **ALFRED MERRITT SMITH WATER TREATMENT FACILITY**, seen jutting out of the arm of land in the foreground, is a direct filtration plant which serves all of southern Nevada, the Las Vegas Valley, and Boulder City. The plant has a capacity of 400 million gallons of water a day.

(*opposite*) Twenty minutes to the east of Las Vegas is the emerging megaresort community **LAKE LAS VEGAS**. With its splendid Jack Nicklaus signature golf course, and more courses to come, lots such as these which extend into the manmade lake are priced in the million-dollar range. When the community is built out, it will have several major hotel/casinos and be a destination resort area unto itself. (*above*) Putting **LAKE LAS VEGAS** into the context of its environs.

(*above and opposite*) Despite significant competition from a number of major gaming companies in Las Vegas, **HOOVER DAM** is the top tourist attraction in southern Nevada. Built between 1931 and 1936 – two years ahead of schedule and under budget – the arch-gravity structure was designed to control flooding and provide hydroelectric power for a number of major western cities. More than a million acres of land in the U.S. and half a million acres in Mexico are irrigated through the benefits of Hoover Dam. The three-and-a-quarter million cubic yards of concrete in the dam would be sufficient to pave a standard highway, 16 feet wide, from San Francisco to New York, or pave over the entire state of Rhode Island.

(*opposite*) **HOOVER DAM** was built in blocks or vertical columns varying in size from about 60 feet square at the upstream face of the dam to about 25 feet square at the downstream face. (*above*) A spectacular new visitors' center (brown building with turquoise dome beyond dam face) was opened in June, 1995, at a cost estimated between $85 and $120 million.

(*above*) A panoramic view of **HOOVER DAM**, neatly wedged into Black Canyon, belies the technological wonder and human life toll exacted by the feat. One hundred seventeen workers died in the construction of the dam. (*opposite*) This section of **LAKE MOHAVE** resembles a giant manta ray. The lake is controlled by Davis Dam, which functions to regulate Colorado River water for delivery to Mexico as required by the Mexican Water Treaty of 1944.

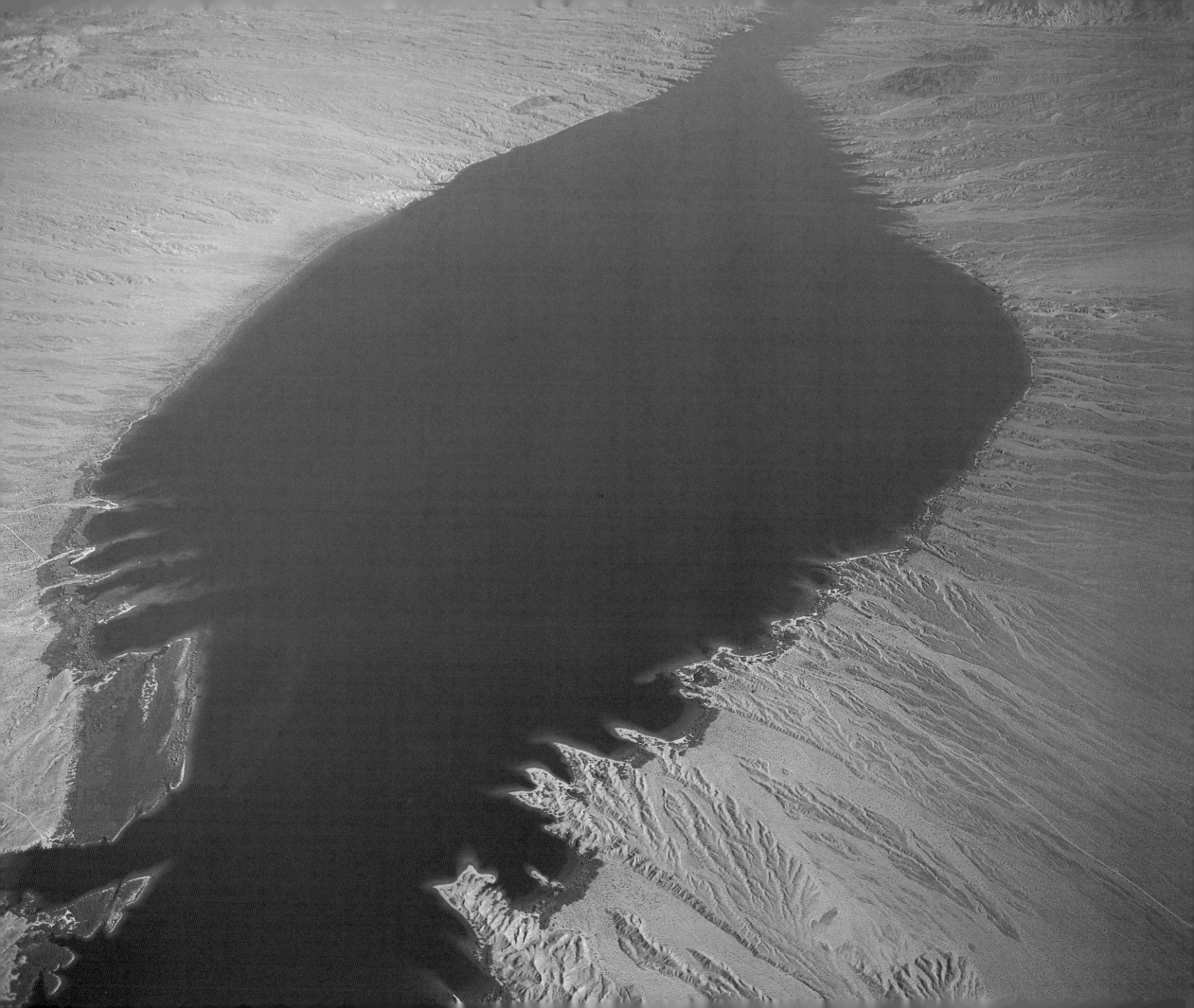

(*opposite*) **LAUGHLIN**, Nevada, left of the Colorado River, and its bedroom community **BULLHEAD CITY**, Arizona, are one of the big stories in legalized gaming in the last decade. By catering to snowbirds, recreational-vehicle aficionados, and budget-conscious gamblers, Laughlin attracted about a dozen of Las Vegas' top casino operators, who built successful properties along the river banks. (*above*) A view from the Arizona side of the river.

In 1984, **LAUGHLIN** had a grand total of 95 residents, temperatures were higher than the population, and there was one casino for every 16 townspeople. Now the area does close to a billion dollars in annual gambling revenue, ranking ahead of Lake Tahoe as the third biggest revenue producer in Nevada. It even has an outstanding golf course, **EMERALD RIVER** (foreground).

DAVIS DAM (center left), in addition to regulating Colorado River water delivery, also protects fish and wildlife, captures and delays flash flood discharges, and provides assistance to downstream irrigators.

THE UTAH CANYONS

(*above*) The **ZION** Canyon region in southwestern Utah is part of an extraordinary landscape network that includes Bryce Canyon, Cedar Breaks, and Capitol Reef. The grandeur extends east into Colorado and south to the Grand Canyon. This fisheye shot shows the rural community of **SPRINGDALE**, Utah, winding its way toward the colossal monoliths that mark the entrance to the canyon. (*opposite*) **SPRINGDALE** was settled in the 1860s by those searching for new lands suitable for irrigation farming. At an elevation of 3,900 feet, the town is the gateway to the south entrance. Once inside the park, elevations reach as high as 7,810 feet.

(*opposite*) The sedimentary rock that forms the walls and slopes of **ZION** comprises a colorful palette of whites, tans, greens, purples, reds, and yellows. But the monumental paintbrush that splashed color across the canyon can play tricks on the eye as the sun moves across the western sky. The colors are dramatically different from morning to afternoon. (*above*) The **ZION** Canyon of today was developed over a few million years, but has been treated as a public treasure only since 1919, when it was declared a national park.

The extreme variety of color, elevation, and topography have drawn artists and photographers to **ZION** for the last century. Closer inspection would reveal an active wildlife population lurking in the cliffs and outcroppings. Over 285 species of birds can be found, as well as cougars, mule deer, rabbits, skunks, water shrew, desert horned lizards, and tiger salamanders.

(*above and opposite*) The city of **MESQUITE**, Nevada, is less than two hours northeast of Las Vegas and has become something of a last-chance gambling opportunity for travelers heading to Utah or Arizona. A couple of resorts; Merv Griffin's Players Island (right) and Si Redd's Oasis (left) – which offers two Arnold Palmer-designed golf courses – spearhead a surging economy.

(*opposite and above*) Writer T.C. Bailey wrote of Utah's **BRYCE CANYON**: "There are deep caverns and rooms resembling ruins of prisons, castles, churches with their guarded walls, battlements, spires and steeples, niches and recesses, presenting the wildest and most wonderful scene that the eye of man ever beheld." They are sometimes called "badlands," other times "God's country," but few would deny that the sculpted walls of Bryce Canyon are an awesome testament to nature's tools – primarily weathering and erosion – and how they've shaped this magnificent spectacle.

(*above*) In **BRYCE**, seemingly unextraordinary terrain runs smack into awesome, ridged walls, which guard the land like a fortress. (*opposite*) Man-made trails wind throughout the inhospitable cliffs. Hikers are not only breathtaken, but often winded as well.

(*opposite and above*) Two more views of **BRYCE** reveal the diversity of the landscape. The plenitude of trees surrounding the walls on all sides makes them appear
more stark, and ultimately more dramatic.

Sometimes, in an unpopulated land, even the richest treasures can go unnoticed, and so it wasn't until 1923 that President Warren Harding yielded to public pressure and proclaimed **BRYCE CANYON** a national monument. Five years later, Congress passed legislation that doubled the size of the monument and gave it national park status. The well-worn road to the canyon suggests its popularity with beauty seekers.

The town of **TROPIC**, two miles east of Bryce Canyon, was created when area residents prior to the turn of the 20th Century completed the digging of a ten-mile ditch that brought water from the Sevier River over the rim and onto their fields below. This ongoing irrigation has created the patchwork of green fields pictured here.

LAS VEGAS WEST

The **U.S. AIR FORCE RADAR INSTALLATION** at **ANGEL PEAK** is located between Kyle Canyon and Lee Canyon on Mount Charleston. It provides communication from the Tonopah Range to Nellis Air Force Base and can even provide microwave air-traffic control assistance for passing aircraft. It is owned and operated by the FAA.

The **LEE CANYON SKI AREA**, on Mount Charleston and just a 45-minute drive from Las Vegas,
allows many southern Nevadans to boast that they have snow-skied and water-skied on the same day.

(*opposite*) Who would suspect that on the same day this photo was taken over the gentle slopes of **LEE CANYON**, thousands of Las Vegas visitors in the valley below were basking under a warm sun by hotel swimming pools? Yet that was the case. (*above*) For southern Nevadans who fear that the blistering desert heat is on the verge of baking them to the texture of earthenware, or for those who just need a break from the visual blight of cactus and sagebrush and have an irrepressible urge to hug a tree, **MOUNT CHARLESTON** is the answer.

139

MOUNT CHARLESTON is part of the Toiyabe National Forest, and the third highest peak in Nevada, at 11,918 feet. On a cloudless day, the desert ranges and canyon lands of northwestern Arizona and southwestern Utah come into view.

(*left*) An expansive view of **MOUNT CHARLESTON**, from its peak down to the Mount Charleston Hotel in the valley (center). (*right*) Only human passageways interrupt the thickly forested hills of ponderosa pines, bristlecone pines, and white firs.

(*opposite*) The other side of **MOUNT CHARLESTON** and the Cold Creek area. Nowhere can one more fully appreciate the miracle of Las Vegas – a community of more than a million residents living in what was once desolation – than from the top of this mountain. (*above*) **SPRING MOUNTAIN RANCH**, west of Las Vegas, has a rich history. It was once owned by radio personality Chester Lauck, also known as Lum, of the *Lum and Abner Show*. He sold it to wealthy Vera Krupp, whose Krupp Diamond was stolen from the ranch and later returned, because it was too famous to fence. The ranch is now owned by the Nevada Park System, which holds summer concerts and musicals there.

(*opposite*) **SPRING MOUNTAIN** is an interesting geological formation, and has a long history in the development of southern Nevada The ranch at its base began as a campsite on the northern route of the Old Spanish Trail. Later on, during a mining boom on nearby Mount Potosi, farmers grew produce there. (n.b. It was on Mount Potosi that actress Carole Lombard, wife of Clark Gable, lost her life in a plane crash in 1942 while on a War Bonds tour.) Years later the ranch was owned by German munitions heiress Vera Krupp, who in turn sold it to Howard Hughes in 1967. (*above*) A geological formation near Spring Mountain resembles a mother dinosaur napping with her baby. Could it have been?

(*above*) To the west of the glittery Strip, equally breathtaking but far more placid, are the vistas of **RED ROCK CANYON**. Hardy souls enjoy climbing the sheer rock walls, but most are content oggling the scenic 13-mile drive through rust-red Aztec sandstone towers. (*opposite*) At certain times of day, the rocks of **RED ROCK** appear impossibly red, but it's all truly natural.

(*above*) The **DESERT SPORTSMAN'S RIFLE & PISTOL CLUB**, on the western edge of Las Vegas, appears from the air as though alien visitors had left a message in the sand (*below*) the **SOUTHERN NEVADA CORRECTIONAL CENTER** prison in Jean, Nevada, (right) doesn't offer much in the way of recreation. But just across the desert there's a lot to do: at **NEVADA LANDING HOTEL AND CASINO** (left of road) and the **GOLD STRIKE HOTEL & GAMBLING HALL** (right of road).

DESPERADO, the world's tallest roller coaster, rides herd at Buffalo Bill's Hotel-Casino, located in the Nevada-California border town of Primm. Although the Eagles' song of the same name is a serene ballad, this Desperado is strictly rock 'n' roll. Traveling at speeds of up to 80 mph for three minutes, passengers experience near-zero gravity three times and a vertical drop of 400 feet.

(*opposite*) The recently renamed bordertown of **PRIMM**, Nevada, (it used to be called Stateline), has become far more than a stopping-off place for California visitors on their way to Las Vegas. With three properties: Buffalo Bill's, Primadonna, and Pistol Pete's, and the thrilling Desperado rollercoaster, it now stages big-name concerts and world-class boxing and is a destination unto itself. (*above*) The town of **MERCURY**, Nevada, sits inauspiciously on the edge of the Nevada Test Site, where nuclear testing has been conducted since 1951. Since late 1962, all atomic tests have been conducted underground. Most of the workers at the test site reside in Mercury when they are on duty.

(above) The **JAMES HARDIE GYPSUM** plant, west of Las Vegas near the Blue Diamond cutoff, has been in operation since 1924 and produces 500,000 tons of gypsum a year. *(opposite)* **PAHRUMP**, Nevada, 90 minutes west of Las Vegas, was first scientifically explored by John C. Fremont as he made his way from Southern California to Utah in 1844. A century and a half later it is a burgeoning community with its own golf course, **CALVADA COUNTRY CLUB** (center).

PAHRUMP VALLEY VINEYARDS, Nevada's only winery, was founded in 1990 and in its first four years of production won 23 gold, silver, and bronze medals in domestic and international competition. The winery produces a white varietal, a blush, a Chardonnay, a Cabernet Sauvignon, and a Burgundy.

McCARRAN INTERNATIONAL AIRPORT is not unlike an international fashion model: attractive, hurried, and always working the runways. In 1995, McCarran handled 30 million passengers, nearly triple the number of just 10 years ago, and is forever undergoing expansion to keep pace with the dynamic city it services.

This undated NASA photograph was definitely taken from **"ABOVE LAS VEGAS,"** – like 13 miles above. Seven or eight golf courses can be seen (the red rectangles), while the current total in 1996 is 29 and counting. Our guess is that the photo was taken in 1962, what's yours?

(*left*) The eclectic home of neurosurgeon and Nevada Lieutenant Governor Lonnie Hammargren has been explored on *Lifestyles of the Rich and Famous*. It has everything from spaceships to replicas of the Thomas and Mack Center and old casino signage. (*below left*) The expansive home (front, center) on the lip of Sunrise Mountain, is said to belong to a well-known movie action hero. The Mormon Temple is in the background. (*below right*) The twin white palaces (center right) bordering Las Vegas Golf Club are home to entertainers Siegfried and Roy and their menagerie of wild animals who perform with them at The Mirage. Many a golfer has been known to back off from his putt at the sound of a lion's roar coming from across the street.

(opposite and above) Just look what's become of a dusty rail-road depot located smack dab in the middle of nowhere.

Page 2

Helicoptering over the **LAS VEGAS STRIP** at night is like being pulled down the tube of a kaleidoscope, the mosaics of explosive color growing ever richer and more resplendent the deeper you go. As legalized gambling has increased in popularity, the stakes for hotel-casino owners on the Strip have skyrocketed as well. Those who don't continually expand, upgrade, or bedazzle are soon lost in the shuffle.

Page 3

MOUNT CHARLESTON: Just 45 minutes northwest of downtown Las Vegas, this 11,918-foot peak offers great hiking and sightseeing in spring and summer, and wonderful skiing in winter. Wildlife such as coyotes, foxes, mule deer, and wild horses are populous, and 27 species of plants can be found here that grow nowhere else on earth.

Page 4

HOOVER DAM sits there in all its majesty, silently taunting all the dreamers and schemers 30 miles away on the Las Vegas Strip to just try and construct something quite so magnificent. Even with exploding volcanoes, sinking pirate ships, pyramids that light up the atmosphere, and the chorus line of the *Folies Bergere*, it remains the top single tourist attraction in southern Nevada.

Page 5

The majestic **GRAND CANYON** was carved by the Colorado River system, which slices through a vertical mile of rock. River water, equipped with its corrosive tools of silt, mud, and cobbles, sliced through the rock layers over 5 million years ago, and over the course of about 4 million years achieved its present depth. Upon his first visit in 1903, President Teddy Roosevelt said: "Leave it as it is . . . the ages have been at work on it, and man can only mar it . . . Keep it for your children, your children's children, and for all who come after you, as the one great sight which every American should see."

Photographs on the dust jacket cover are *(left to right)* **THE GRAND CANYON, LAS VEGAS** and **MOUNT CHARLESTON**. Photograph on the dust jacket back cover is **HOOVER DAM.**